THORNS, HORNS, AND CRESCENT MOONS

Reading and Writing
Nature Poems

compiled and annotated by Jill Kalz

PICTURE WINDOW BOOKS
a capstone imprint

Special thanks to our adviser for his expertise:

Terry Flaherty, PhD, Professor of English
Minnesota State University, Mankato

Editor: Jill Kalz
Designer: Lori Bye
Art Director: Nathan Gassman
Production Specialist: Kathy McColley

Illustration Credits
Cristian Bernardini, 4, 5, 8, 11, 12-13, 14, 24, 28, 29, 32; Dustin Burkes-Larrañaga, cover, 1, 7, 9, 25; Sandra D'Antonio, 15, 20-21, 31;
Matt Loveridge, back cover, 2-3, 22, 23, 26-27; Simon Smith, 6, 10, 16, 18; Tou Yia Xiong, 17, 19

Picture Window Books are published by Capstone,
1710 Roe Crest Drive, North Mankato, Minnesota 56003
www.capstonepub.com

Library of Congress Cataloging-in-Publication Data
Cataloging-in-publication information is on file with the Library of Congress.
ISBN 978-1-4795-2197-5 (library binding)
ISBN 978-1-4795-2948-3 (paperback)
ISBN 978-1-4795-3331-2 (eBook PDF)

Printed in the United States of America in Brainerd, Minnesota.
092013   007770BANGS14

TABLE OF CONTENTS

DISCOVER THE POET IN YOU

Nature touches you in some way every day. *Every day!* You might not even see your friends every day! But the sun greets you. Wind moves the trees. Insects buzz. Birds soar. And no two people experience these things in exactly the same way. You can share how autumn rain feels on your face by writing a poem. Share how a peach tastes, how seaweed smells.

WHY WRITE POETRY?

When you write poetry, you're an explorer. You discover new words, new combinations of words, and new meanings. You use old words in fresh ways. Poetry opens your ears. Sentences can play like music. Poetry opens your eyes. It's as if you're seeing the world around you—your ordinary, everyday world—for the very first time. Poetry can be a new language that allows you to share your ideas and experiences.

WHAT TOOLS DOES A POET USE?

Whether you're building a house, a car, or a video game, you need tools to get the job done. Poets use tools to build their poems too. Their tools include parts of speech (such as nouns, verbs, and adjectives), ways of writing (like different forms or types of poetry), and the cool sounds that letters and words make when they're combined (like rhymes and repeated letters). Knowing what the tools are and how to use them is what this book is all about.

HOW DO I READ THIS BOOK?

Start by reading the poems. All of them are about nature. After you read each one, take a look at the Info Box on the bottom of the page. There you'll find definitions of poetic forms and tools. You may also find helpful tips, questions to consider, or writing prompts. Near the back of the book, you'll have the chance to review what you've learned and practice writing your own poems. Before you know it, you'll be a poet!

The Owl

Perched on a thick branch
the owl blinks then scans the ground
for toads in the night.

—Connie Colwell Miller

DO YOU HAIKU?

A **haiku** is a Japanese form of poetry. It has three lines and follows a 5-7-5 pattern of **syllables**. Lines 1 and 3 have five syllables. Line 2 has seven. The poem above is short, but it tells us a lot. For starters, we learn that an owl is awake. What else do we learn?

Mushroom Gloom

Down in the mulberry bog,
Sat a mushroom alone in the fog.
He said with a sigh,
"I am a fungi,
But I'm doomed to be stuck on a log."

—Christopher L. Harbo

SOUNDS LIKE ...

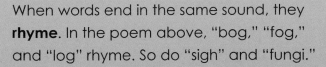

When words end in the same sound, they **rhyme**. In the poem above, "bog," "fog," and "log" rhyme. So do "sigh" and "fungi."

Rhyming words can add interest and structure to a poem. What other rhymes can you find in this poem?

Sidewalk Worms

The sidewalk's surface slowly squirms
With at least 12 dozen worms.

The morning rains that coaxed them up
Have now gone dry and left them stuck.

And as they wriggle to and fro
I wonder where they hope to go.

For when the sun climbs up the sky
Its heat will doom these worms to fry.

But have no fear, do not despair.
Nature's cruel, but I still care.

I'll spend my morning, noon, and night
Saving earthworms from their plight.

I'll pluck them up and gently pass
Them into blades of cool, damp grass.

And when my work is all complete
They'll live once more beneath my feet.

—Christopher L. Harbo

FEEL THE BEAT

Rhythm is the "drum" in poetry. It can be created by **beats** or syllables. You can measure rhythm in **meter**—just count the beats or stressed syllables in each line. Tap the beats with your finger: "The SIDE-walk's SUR-face SLOW-ly SQUIRMS ..."

Red-Tailed Hawk

hawk
red, rust
soaring, searching, diving
wings, talons, whiskers, paws
scurrying, squeaking, escaping
lucky, breathless
mouse

—Connie Colwell Miller

WHAT A GEM

The diamond-shaped **diamante** uses a parts-of-speech pattern. The seven-line poem starts with a noun. Two adjectives and three verbs follow. Next come four nouns, three verbs, and two adjectives. The final noun is often the opposite of the first.

9

The First Snowfall

Hard, cold
rains lighten to
white, shimmering crystals.
Like a blanket, the snow covers
us. Hush.

—Jennifer Fandel

A **cinquain** (sin-CANE) is a five-line poem. "Cinq" means "five" in French. The poem follows a 2-4-6-8-2 pattern of syllables.

Count the syllables in the poem above with your fingers. Feel the pattern? Count with your fingers when you write too. It'll help!

Quercus velutina

Ogre warts and knobby joints,
Aged-leather leaf litter,
Kickstand of unseen roots,
Trunk furrowed with rippling bark
Rising tall from dark, rich soil,
Earth's fist punching skyward with
Explosions of meaty, helmeted acorns
Showering down like cannon fire

—Jeni Wittrock

HIDDEN MESSAGES

An **acrostic** is a poem that's twice as nice. When the first letter of each line is put together, it spells another word or phrase. Sometimes that hidden message is the poem's main idea or title of the poem. Try writing an acrostic using your first name.

The Icicle

On a frigid winter afternoon
My best bud, Jim, and I
Walk past the county courthouse
When a bright glint strikes my eye.

The sunshine bounces off a shaft
Of ice so clear and clean
I know it is an icicle
Unlike any I've ever seen.

This crystal pillar calls to us
It must be 10 feet long.
We whack it with our mittens
But its base is thick and strong.

WHAT HAPPENED?

12

Narrative poems tell stories. They may be long or short, rhyming or not. The stories may be simple or complex. They may include action and **dialogue**. What details does this poet use to build excitement and keep you interested in the poem's story?

Then I notice Jim's reflection
In the icicle's bright sheen.
A grin has spread across his face—
His eyes look sharp and keen.

"I bet it tastes like dew," he says,
"Or a bubbling mountain spring.
One lick should test my theory.
I've just got to taste this thing!"

"That's not a good idea," I say,
"Please, Jim, don't press your luck."
But he doesn't heed my warning
And now his tongue is stuck.

—Christopher L. Harbo

This Is Why I Love Swimming Pools

I'm doggy-paddling past the dock when something grabs my ankles.

It feels like flocks of lovesick eels—the seaweed's out to get me.

My peaceful back float's ruined again by clingy plumes of green.

Wet witch's hair, a swimmer-snare—the seaweed's out to get me.

By the shoreline, ankle deep, I'm wading, picking shells. Just one misstep—

my foot's in mush. I swear, the seaweed's out to get me!

—Jeni Wittrock

SEE THIS?

A **concrete poem** is a picture as well as a poem. The words form the shape of the poem's subject. See how the lines in the poem above talk about seaweed and look like seaweed too? Try writing a concrete poem about a snowman or the moon.

Mosquito

I am snoozing, snoozing happily
when a buzzing fills my ears.
First it's here. Then it's there.
I swat. I slap. I clap.
The buzzing pauses. All is still.
But then it buzzes more.
The noise! It hovers near my neck,
its motor droning on. This pesky pest,
this little insect drives me crazy until dawn.

—Connie Colwell Miller

JOYFUL NOISE

Not all rhymes happen at the ends of lines. Sometimes they happen within lines. These **internal rhymes** create a fun echo of sound.

Hear the "ears / here," "slap / clap," and "motor / droning" rhymes in the poem above? What other rhymes can you find?

The Story of Rivers

Rain and melting snow make a river grow.
Unlike lakes, a river never stands still.
Gravity makes its waters travel downhill.
Around the world, people watch rivers flow.

A river cuts a channel through the ground.
Starting at a source, ending at a mouth,
rivers can flow from east, west, north, or south,
traveling straight or wandering around.

Rivers help the growth of each plant and seed.
Their waters let us bathe, swim, cook, and drink.
Don't pollute it. Don't waste it. Stop and think.
Rivers hold the water that people need.

The next time you sit along a river's bank,
remember, its waters are there to thank.

—Jennifer Fandel

MAKING PICTURES

Imagery is what you picture in your mind when you read a poem. Details like colors, sounds, textures, smells, and flavors all help create imagery. In this poem, the poet uses action verbs such as "cut," "flow," "wander," and "swim" to help us picture the river.

Great Blue Heron

Where are you, Great Blue?
Hard to spot
in the tall-grass swamp,
you walk softly, slowly
on legs so boney.

You search for a fat crustacean
or a fish to spear for lunch
and—*Freeze!*

A fat crab clambers
through the sandy water.
You calculate where
your sharp beak needs to stab.
There! Now!

Your head and beak move fast.
You grab a tasty crab.

Oh, gray Great Blue,
you are still hungry and need
a bigger swamp to feed you.

You launch, lift, take off ...

Your long neck curves,
your legs dangle
and your fringed wings sing
soft songs.

—Jennifer Fandel

SAME SOUNDS

Poets use **alliteration** to create interest
in a poem. Alliteration repeats leading
consonant sounds that are the same.

In the poem above, "crab clambers" and
"sing soft songs" are examples of alliteration.
See if you can find at least two more.

17

A Little Help?

On a walk across this dry land
I stepped in a pool of quicksand.
I've sunk past my nose.
I hate to impose.
Could someone please lend me a hand?

—Christopher L. Harbo

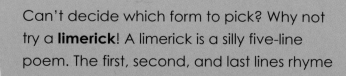
RHYME TIME

Can't decide which form to pick? Why not try a **limerick**! A limerick is a silly five-line poem. The first, second, and last lines rhyme ("land / quicksand / hand"). The third and fourth lines are shorter and rhyme with each other ("nose / impose").

A Sycamore Lullaby

Under the shade of the sycamore tree,
    the spotted, mottled sycamore tree,
whose bark peels and reveals
    smooth whites and yellows and grays

you can dream of swinging on
    its tall branches,
you can sway with the swish
    of its green leaves.

It stands straight and tall,
reaching toward the sun, and at night
glowing in the starshine
    and the moonlight.

—Jennifer Fandel

STICKING TOGETHER

A **stanza** is a group of lines that is usually separated by a blank line, called a **stanza break**. Stanzas often contain complete thoughts or images. In this poem, the first two stanzas are one long sentence. The stanza break creates a pause.

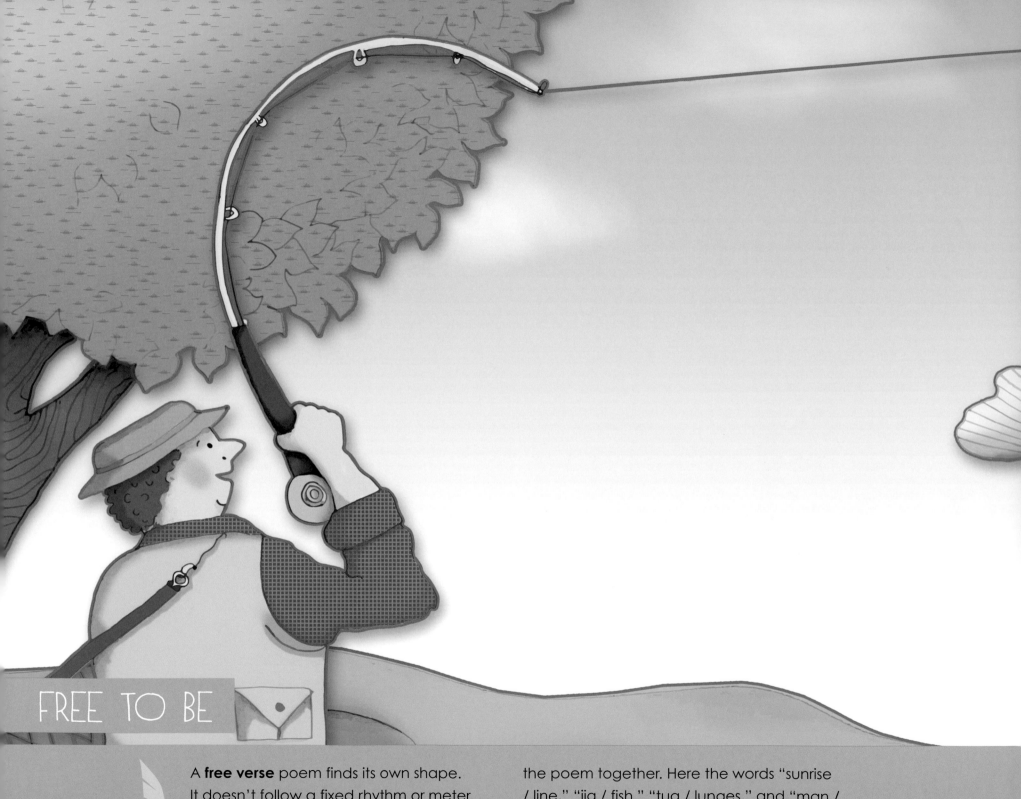

FREE TO BE

A **free verse** poem finds its own shape. It doesn't follow a fixed rhythm or meter. Repeating sounds or words may help hold the poem together. Here the words "sunrise / line," "jig / fish," "tug / lunges," and "man / branch" create pleasing echoes.

Fishing

Just where the morning sun
flashes on the water, the shiny
mouth of a fish breaks through.
The fisherman's muscles twitch.
The man watches as the green O plucks
a water bug from the face
of the lake, leaving only ripples
and air. The fisherman
casts, his brown arm reaching
toward the sunrise as the line
unspools with a zing. The jig and hook
plop softly into the lake,
not far from where the fish nabbed
its snack. The fisherman reels surely,
trolling the jig and, in his mind's eye,
he sees the fish as it wriggles below,
swimming into position to swallow the lure.
This is what the fisherman sees
when he feels a soft tug. Like an animal,
the fisherman lunges: He yanks the rod,
sets the hook, locks his knees. When the fish
takes off, the pole bows like a branch
in a storm, and the two of them—a man and a fish—
wrestle it out in the orange morning light.

—Connie Colwell Miller

Lyric of a Sunflower

I am a lonely sunflower
Locked in your solar grip.
I bloom to soak in all your power
And track your daily trip
From east to west across the land
Absorbing each sweet ray—
Your light provides a steady hand,
To guide me through the day.
But when at twilight you descend
And darkness slowly creeps.
I follow you right to the end,
Then bow my head to weep.

—Christopher L. Harbo

ALMOST HUMAN

When poets use **personification**, they make non-human things seem human. Real plants don't feel sadness or longing, but in the poem above, they do. This sunflower is lonely. And it cries too! See if you can personify a toaster or a honeybee.

A Bright Surprise

I wander and ramble
on my happy, fast feet.
Through the woods and brambles
I wonder what I'll meet.

I thought I might be scared
by a creature with horns.
Squinting in the sun's glare,
I back right into thorns.

Bright red drips down my shin.
Would I get myself loose?
More red covers my skin.
And it tastes like juice!

Berries on the branches
hang, taste both sweet and tart.
Each raspberry dances
in sunlight like small hearts.

Scratched by thorny sticks
at the edge of the woods,
I eat and bend and pick.
And it tastes so good!

—Jennifer Fandel

COUNT TO FOUR

A stanza with four lines is called a **quatrain**. The poem above is made of rhyming quatrains that follow an ABAB pattern.

The ends of the first and third lines rhyme ("ramble / brambles"). So do the second and fourth lines ("feet / meet").

Ode to the Mouse in My Bedroom

There is a mouse in my room.
Can you hear the scratching?
My mother screeched and grabbed the broom,
but I am hoping I can catch him.
Dad set out cheese. I ate it up.
I couldn't let Dad nab him.
Dad set a trap. I broke its hinge,
so I'm the one to grab him.

Truth be told, I need this mouse
for hatching my next scheme.
I can't let Mom swat him to death,
nor Dad smash in his bean.
I hope to wear my parents down
bit by bit by bit.
Then I'll catch the mouse myself
and pitch a giant fit.

I'll hold the mouse up by its tail,
and threaten to let up.
I'll tell my folks, "I'll take him out,
if we can get a pup!"

—Connie Colwell Miller

HOW I FEEL

An **ode** is a type of **lyric poem**. It's usually written in three stanzas of varying line length. Like all lyric poems, odes are personal and full of strong feelings. Why is it so important for the speaker in this poem, and not Mom or Dad, to catch the mouse?

Visiting the Buffalo

In the gulley, a buffalo looms,
a bull with a head the size of a boulder.

His great black haunches sway slowly
from side to side as he lumbers toward the creek.

A thick ebony horn sprouts from each
side of his bulging brow. As he turns

one last time to watch us go, his eyes, each
larger than a cupped palm, are warm and sad.

—Connie Colwell Miller

TWO BY TWO

A pair of poetry lines is called a **couplet**. The lines usually rhyme, but, as shown above, they don't have to. A couplet often stands as a unit, making its own image or point. What is the main image of each couplet in the poem above?

The Ballad of Grog Frog

Gather round, my tadpoles,
And listen as I tout
The ballad of the Grog Frog
And his famous boxing bout.

This tale began at midnight
Beneath a crescent moon
As water lapped the sandy beach
Of Finnegan's Lagoon.

Old Grog Frog was a-strolling
No care did cloud his mind
When a diamond-spotted rattler
Surprised him from behind.

"What's this?" the rattler lisped
While licking scaly lips.
"You'll make a tasty morsel
Once I get you in my grips."

Now Grog Frog didn't flinch a bit
At that cool serpent's voice.
He spun around and simply said,
"I'll give to you a choice.

"Let me live this night, my friend,
And you'll live longer too.
Or risk your skin on one last meal,
The decision's up to you."

The snake hissed, "You talk tough.
But I, sir, know my role."
Then he lunged in like a cracking whip
And swallowed Grog Frog whole.

But Grog Frog was a pro
Who'd never lost a fight
He started throwing punches—
First a left hook, then a right.

The rattler moaned, "Oh, dear me!
My guts are feeling queasy.
I really thought a frog like you
Would slide down nice and easy."

"You were wrong," Grog replied,
"Now take my kind suggestion.
Spit me out before my fists
Bring deadly indigestion."

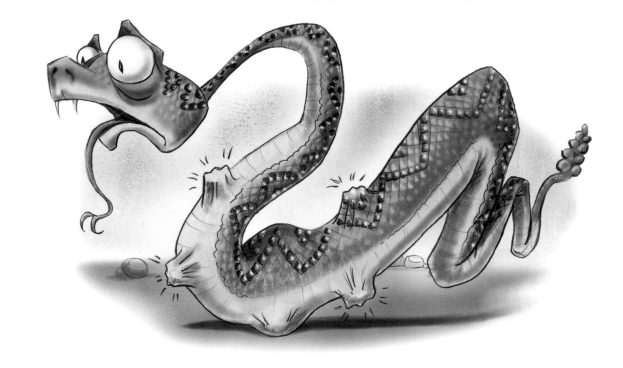

In a flash, the serpent urped—
His insides felt much lighter—
Before him stood the world's
Greatest amphibian prizefighter.

"We've had our sport," the boxer said,
"But clearly I'm the winner.
From here on out, I do advise
You watch what you call dinner."

And that is how—my tadpoles—
The Grog Frog won his bout
With an overeager rattler
Who he fought from inside out.

—Christopher L. Harbo

TELLING TALES

A **ballad** tells a story, usually about a hero or a memorable event. It often contains action, dialogue, and a rhyming pattern.

Long ago, ballads weren't written down. They were shared by word of mouth. As a result, ballads often changed over time.

PRACTICE IT! •

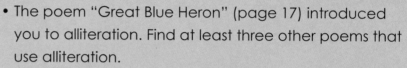

Starting to understand the tools poets use? There are lots of them! The following questions will help you practice with a few tools first before you sit down to write. (Hint: Find a word you don't understand? Look in the Glossary on page 30.)

• When words end in the same sound, they rhyme, such as in the poem "Sidewalk Worms" on page 8. Find other poems in this book that have rhyming lines. Do the rhymes always appear in a pattern?

• On page 14, the poem "This Is Why I Love Swimming Pools" repeats the phrase "the seaweed's out to get me!" Can you find other poems that use the tool of **repetition**?

• In "The Ballad of Grog Frog" (page 26), the poet separates groups of lines and ideas with stanzas. Find other poems that use stanzas.

• The poem "Great Blue Heron" (page 17) introduced you to alliteration. Find at least three other poems that use alliteration.

• You can get a good picture of a poem because of imagery. Which poems created good pictures in your mind? What were some of the details in those poems?

• You read in "A Bright Surprise" (page 23) that raspberries dance "like small hearts" because of **similes**. Similes make comparisons by saying one thing is *like* another. **Metaphors**, on the other hand, make comparisons without the use of the words "like" or "as." Find another poem that uses a simile to help describe something.

28

WRITE IT!

Here's an activity that will help you discover the poet in you!

GO ON A POETRY HIKE

Step into the great outdoors. Any place where you're sure to see animals, plants, or other natural elements will do. Visit a farm, a zoo, the neighborhood park, or your own backyard to find ideas for poems.

1) GET A PEN AND A NOTEBOOK.

2) START WALKING.

Pay close attention to everything around you. Use all your senses: sight, hearing, smell, touch, and taste. Stop once in a while and close your eyes. Doing so may help you hear or smell things more clearly.

3) PICK SOMETHING YOU'D LIKE TO WRITE ABOUT.

Let's say you pick a pigeon. Watch it for awhile, and make a list of everything you notice.

- What does it look like? What colors do you see, and what do those colors remind you of? Describe the bird's size and shape. How does it move?
- Does the pigeon behave or look like a person? Could it?
- What does it eat? Seeds? Crackers? Bits of hot dog bun? How do you think the food tastes?
- How does the pigeon sound?
- Where does it live? Are there other animals around? How to they act toward the pigeon?

4) WHEN YOU'RE DONE, READ THROUGH YOUR LIST.

Choose three things you really like—things you can see and remember clearly. Then try writing a poem about the pigeon. If you get stuck, use one of the poems from the book as an example. "Red-Tailed Hawk" (page 9) might be useful if you're writing a diamante. If you want to write a limerick, check out "Mushroom Gloom" (page 7).

GLOSSARY ●●●●●●●●●●●●●●●●●●●●●●●●●●●●●●●●●

acrostic—a poem that uses the first letters of each line to spell out a word, name, or phrase relating to the poem's topic

alliteration—the use of two or more words that start with the same letter sound

ballad—a rhythmic poem that tells a story and is often sung

beat—a stressed word or syllable in a line of poetry

cinquain—a five-line poem that follows a 2-4-6-8-2 pattern of syllables

concrete poem—a poem that takes the shape of its subject

couplet—a pair of rhyming lines that usually have the same number of beats; couplets make their own point, create a separate image, or summarize the idea of a poem

dialogue—the words spoken between two or more characters (people or creatures); in writing, dialogue is set off with quotation marks

diamante—a seven-line poem that forms a diamond shape and follows this pattern: 1 noun, 2 adjectives, 3 verbs, 4 nouns, 3 verbs, 2 adjectives, 1 noun

free verse—a poem that follows no set rhythm or meter

haiku—a three-line poem that follows a 5-7-5 pattern of syllables

imagery—language that creates pictures in a reader's mind

internal rhyme—a word within a line of poetry that sounds like another word either at the end of the same line or within another line

limerick—a silly five-line poem in which the first two lines rhyme with the last line, and the third and fourth lines rhyme with each other

lyric poem—a poem that expresses strong, personal feelings; sonnets, odes, and elegies are examples of lyric poetry

metaphor—a figure of speech that compares different things without using words such as "like" or "as"

meter—the pattern of beats in each line of a poem

narrative poem—a poem that tells a story

ode—a type of lyric poem, usually written in three stanzas with varying line lengths

personification—giving human characteristics, or traits, to something that isn't human

quatrain—a four-line group of poetry

repetition—saying or doing something again and again

rhyme—word endings that sound the same

rhythm—a pattern of beats, like in music

simile—a figure of speech that compares different things by using the words "like" or "as"

stanza—a grouping of lines in poetry

stanza break—the blank line that separates stanzas in a poem

syllable—a unit of sound in a word

READ MORE

Fandel, Jennifer. *You Can Write Cool Poems.* You Can Write. North Mankato, Minn.: Capstone Press, 2012.

Katz, Bobbi, selected by. *More Pocket Poems.* New York: Dutton Children's Books, 2009.

Kennedy, Caroline, selected by. *Poems to Learn by Heart.* New York: Disney Hyperion Books, 2012.

Prelutsky, Jack. *Pizza, Pigs, and Poetry: How to Write a Poem.* New York: Greenwillow Books, 2008.

Salas, Laura Purdie. *Picture Yourself Writing Poetry: Using Photos to Inspire Writing.* See It, Write It. Mankato, Minn.: Capstone Press, 2012.

LOOK FOR ALL THE BOOKS IN THE SERIES:

PUCKS, CLUBS, AND BASEBALL GLOVES: READING AND WRITING SPORTS POEMS

THORNS, HORNS, AND CRESCENT MOONS: READING AND WRITING NATURE POEMS

TICKLES, PICKLES, AND FLOOFING PERSNICKLES: READING AND WRITING NONSENSE POEMS

TRUST, TRUTH, AND RIDICULOUS GOOFS: READING AND WRITING FRIENDSHIP POEMS

INTERNET SITES

FactHound offers a safe, fun way to find Internet sites related to this book. All of the sites on FactHound have been researched by our staff.

Here's all you do:
Visit www.facthound.com
Type in this code: 9781479521975

Super-cool stuff! Check out projects, games and lots more at www.capstonekids.com